Echoes of Moore Street

DUBLIN WIT

Wisdom Wickedness Banter and Bitching

Paul Ryan

Cartoons: Tom Mathews

THE O'BRIEN PRESS
DUBLIN

First published 1986 by The O'Brien Press
20 Victoria Road, Dublin 6, Ireland.

British Library Cataloguing in Publication Data
Ryan, Paul
Echoes of Moore Street: Dublin wit,
wisdom, wickedness, banter and bitching.
1. English wit and humour
I. Title
828'.91407'08   PN6175

ISBN 0-86278-103-5

10 9 8 7 6 5 4 3

Book design: Michael O'Brien.
Cover design: Jole Bortoli.
Typesetting: Phototype-Set Ltd., Dublin.
Printed in Great Britain by
Billing & Sons Ltd, Worcester

Contents

Banter and Bitching 5

Buying and Selling 10

Children 13

Christmas 15

Compliments 16

Customers 17

Daily Life 24

Fashion 26

Fish 29

Goin' for a Jar 31

Good Advice 35

Health and Hygiene 37

Insults and Threats 39

Law 42

Love and Marriage 43

Love Thy Neighbour 46

Me Husband 51

Pass-remarkable 53

Pleasures of Life 54

Pregnancy 55

Romance 57

Trials and Tribulations 59

Weather 60

Dublin Slang 61

Not the full shilling!

That wan is yapping on an' on all bleedin' morning. Jaysus, whoever turned her on must have gone away and forgotten to come back and turn her off.

Ah it's only poor Annie talking to herself again. The poor soul, she must get terrible stupid answers.

Mary asked me to keep an eye on her stall 'cos she wants to go and get a bikini for her holidays in Spain. I told her with the size of her now, that she'd better get a three-piece one.

Bridie, can ye watch me stall for about half an hour? I'm just going down to O'Connor's the jewellers. I heard the other day you can have your ears pierced there while ye wait.

Look here, I'm tired of doing double the work at this stall, yours as well as me own.
That's strange, luv, cause I do shag all.

Where's young Jacinta this afternoon luv? Is she not helping ye out?
No, luv, it's another of her afternoons off. I'll tell ye something, if she asks for another afternoon off she'll have all her mornings off as well.

You're a bit down today, Chrissie, what's up with ye?
Well, I'm wondering that as I get older will I start to lose me looks?
Well, ye will, luv, if ye'r lucky.

I don't think I look forty-two, Bridie, do I?
No, luv, but ye used to.

Me hair is starting to fall out, can you suggest anything to keep it in?
How about a cardboard box?

You should keep your hair natural like mine, Maisie.
Jaysus, if I'd kept me hair natural like yours I'd be bald.

Hey, Mary, you've a Roman nose and it's roamin all over yer face.
Well, luv, you've a grand nose yourself now, and I'd say that it's handpicked.

Are them pearls real, Mary, give us a look.
Hey, you're biting them.
No, luv, they're not real.
And how would you know anyway with yer false teeth.

I'd better get down to the pawn, Rosie, I hear that customers who left things over thirty days are to be disposed of.

Bridie, ye should have seen the artificial plants in Clerys, they're so lifelike they're unreal.

There's Mary now, standing around and still no sale on them flowers and what with the broken blossoms under her feet wouldn't she remind you of the Little Flower?
Indeed, luv, the little cauliflower.

Oh, she's very into astrology and the stars now. She asked me this morning what sign I was conceived under. What did you tell her? I told her it was Keep off the Grass.

Sacred Heart of the Crucified Jesus, what was that loud bang over at Bridie's stall? Oh, don't worry, luv, it's probably only one of her earrings that's after fallin' off and hittin' the ground.

That oul' rip knows all that's goin' on, she has her nose always to the ground — it's worse than a dachshound's balls.

**Wouldn't ye think she'd take off some of the oul' cardigans now on a lovely fine day like this.
Jaysus, luv, them jumpers is part of her body at this stage, sure if she took any of them off now wouldn't her rib cage collapse?**

Katie is great fun to talk to, she can't say anything nice about anyone.
Yea, she's not prejudiced, she just hates everybody.

She says she's going to have her palm read tonight out in Bray.
Sure, what would they want looking at her palm for, luv, when there are a lot more lines on her face.

The last time the fortune teller told her that she'd be very unhappy until she was forty but that after that she'd get used to it.

Do ye want to hear me bird impression, Bridie?
Very good, luv, but be careful now that ye don't fly away and start to eat worms.

Have you put the kettle on yet, Maisie?
I tried to, luv, but I couldn't get me arm through the spout.

Can you take the flowers out of that box, missus?

Certainly, son, which ones would youse like?

Oh, I don't want any, I just thought that some of them looked a bit tired.

Ye'r in great humour today, Christy, that song ye'r singing used to be a lovely tune.

Hey, Bridie, I'll have to marry ye soon, 'cause I can't sleep at night thinking of all the money ye'r making there on that stall.

Oh, dream on, luv, dream on.

I've heard that ye'r givin' up the stall, that ye've loads of money now.

Oh, indeed, I've enough money to last me a lifetime, that's if I don't spend anything.

Do you want a ride on me Suzuki?

Jaysus, I never heard it called that before.

Young wan, how's yer mother for coal blocks?

She's very slack, luv.

Mary asked me to mind her stall for a few minutes so that she could go off and buy a bit of make-up for tonight. I'd a good mind to tell her to go down to Lenehans instead and get a bag of Polyfilla to fill in her cracks.

Have ye got a paper, son?
There ye are, mister.
Are ye sure, now, this isn't
  yesterday's?
Careful, now, or ye might be in
  tomorrow's yerself.

**Excuse me, missus, do you do
  the pools?**
**Oh no, sir, it's not me, it's the
  dog.**

Is Joe around, missus? No,
  luv, I'm afraid Joe passed away
  last week.
Well, I never, he didn't mention
  anything about a wheel barra,
  did he?

I've been trying to think of a
  word now for two weeks.
How about a fortnight, luv?

Hey, Mary, did ye get me
  washing powder, me packet of
  Tide?
Oh no, luv, he said he was
  waiting for it to come in.

**I believe that wan's so near-
  sighted that she can't make
  people out till they're on top
  of her.**

Yer man's a right eejit. I asked
  him what would he do if a
  foreigner tried to rape his sister
  and do you know what he said
  to me?
Wha'?
He said he'd try and get in
  between them.

I'm not surprised to hear that yer
  wan can't see through them
  glasses, luv, sure didn't she take
  them over when her granny
  died.

**Didn't Charlie catch the two
  of them in bed together.
  What are ye doin' there?
  says he to the missus. Jaysus,
  luv, didn't I tell ye all along
  that he was stupid.**

Oh, he says he won't leave them
  anythin'. Sure he's so mean that
  he'd live in yer ear and sub-let
  yer eardrum. Ye know, he'll
  probably turn it into travellers'
  cheques and take it with him.

**That wan is as deaf as a
  door. The doctor examined
  her and told her that she
  had an insufficient passage
  and that if she heard
  anything it'd be a miracle.
  Well, she was as white as a
  maggot. She thought he said
  that she had a fish in her
  passage and that if she had
  anything it would be a
  mackerel, now I ask ye.**

Oh, as deaf as a post. When the
  justice told her that she could
  have free legal aid, she thought
  she was going to get a glass of
  Lucozade.

I don't need any court, says she. The only barrister I need is the one to hold up me stairs and that the children can slide off.

That poor oul' wan is so unfortunate that if it was raining soup she'd be out with a fork.

I don't know how yer wan manages to do so many bleedin' stupid things in the one day.
I think she must get up early, luv.

Oh, she's so stupid I told her this morning that I was thinking of backing that horse each way. Oh, she says to me, I thought they only ran the one way.

That wan's so thick she thinks her menstural cycle is some kind of Honda.

Look at that, late again this mornin'. Jaysus, that wan would be late for her own funeral.
Oh, it must be her back trouble.
Yea, I'd say she has great trouble gettin' it off the bed.

The bitch still isn't speaking to you? But I thought you'd made yer mind up not to talk to her.
Yea, but she didn't speak to me to give me a chance not to talk to her.

You know she's that stupid that she took back the pill and told the doctor it was the wrong size, that it kept fallin' out.

Oh, that wan and the goin's on of her, sure she's past redemption.
Well, I'll say this much for her — she makes a lot of mistakes but they're different every time.
She was born stupid and she has had several relapses.

I tell ye, that one's as ignorant as a bag of arses. Pushed and shoved past me she did.
Oh, she'd no call to do that. But I wouldn't mind her, luv, sure there's no point in being ignorant unless ye can show it.

She's as tough as an ox, when she dies they'll make Bovril outa her.

I see she has the hump again.
Jaysus, she's worse than any camel.

Wouldn't ye think she'd open her mouth when she'd smile at ye. Ye know I don't think I've ever seen her teeth. Ye might as well be greeted by a slit in a carrot.

Well, the oul' dry stick, ye know it pains her to salute a body. When I greet her I get no warmth at all in her oul' hello.
No, luv, but I'd say now when she's talking to you there's plenty of warmth in her goodbye.

*I'm telling ye, luv, what I had
to go through this morning,
half of them undecided as to
what they wanted and the
other half who couldn't
make up their minds. I'm
telling ye, if Christ was
working down here he'd ask
to be crucified quick.*

Well, I'll tell ye, Bridie, that
wan this morning really had
me annoyed, fingering the
oranges, sniffing the apples
and, finally, doesn't she go
over and feel a cucumber for
ages.
What did ye say to her, luv?
I said, Pardon me, missus, it
doesn't get bigger if ye feel
it.

Did ye see that wan the way she
was prodding and poking at
them vegetables. The oul' bitch
didn't know what she wanted.
No, luv, but by the way she
swept some of them aside she
certainly knew what she didn't
want.

Didn't I catch her trying to
slip the fruit into the pram
in under the babby. Oh, I
didn't mean any harm, says
she, I didn't mean any harm.
You didn't mean any harm!
says I. Well, I bet now that
Hitler said the same thing.

*Jaysus, says I. Oh, the holy
name again, says he. Now,
you'll have to stop all that
language and swearing, says
he. Remember the second of
the Lord's commandments –
thou shalt not take the name
of the Lord thy God in vain.
Excuse me, now, says I, ye
needn't start throwing the
commandments at me. I've
always known how to
conduct meself, and as for
swearing, anyway, the man's
name was Jesus.*

Well, Mary, when I think of the
night I was going home and this
cur stops me in Frederick Street
and asks me for a lift. Jaysus,
luv, I wouldn't mind but I was
walking at the time.

Well, there he was, staring
and staring at me, and he so
cross-eyed that his right eye
should be where his left one
is.

So I says to her, now you're the
most popular sweet seller on the
street, Katie, what's yer secret?
Well, says she, the rest of youse
scoop up more than a pound of
sweets and then start taking
away. Well, I always scoop up
less than a pound and then add
to it. So there ye are.

Them two wanted flowers for the first communion, red carnations one wanted. I'm sorry, luv, says I, I've only these white ones left now.

Oh, that won't do at all, says she, they have to be red. Well what do you expect me to do, luv, says I, shed me life's blood over them?

This fella comes over to me. Is it possible to buy half a head of cabbage, madam? says he. Oh, I'll have to ask the boss about that, says I, quickly. So I goes over to Paddy and I says, Paddy there's an oul' stupid ghet over there who wants to buy half a head of cabbage. Well, merciful Jesus, didn't I turn round and there he was right behind me.

What did ye do?

Oh, says I, and this nice gentleman will have the other half.

As I told you before, Bridie, that Nora is as deaf as a post. I was shouting across to May this morning saying that the cabbage was 'this big' and that the cucumbers were 'that large' and I making the gestures to show her the size, when over Nora comes to me and says, Oh I know that fella ye'r talking about, he lives over in Sheriff Street.

When me mother died she left me this stall.

Well, them things are so stale she must have left ye everything that's on it as well.

Isn't her babby lovely, Bridie?
He looks just like his father.
Wouldn't it be better now,
luv, if the child looked more
like her husband.

---

*She got a bit confused with
all the babies there. I think,
says she, I'll keep this fella,
sure he's in a better pram
than me own.*

Why has she the babby in such a
high pram?
So that she can hear him when
he falls out, luv.

What did they call the child?
Hazel.
Hazel!
Yea, with all the lovely saints'
names around they had to
go and call her after a
bleedin' nut.

---

*Marie says she'd love a
family.
Tell her she's welcome to
mine any time.
How many have you got now,
Sadie?
Six children, luv, that's
including me husband.*

. . . and how many have ye now,
missus?
Five boys, missus. God, would ye
feel it, sure ye wouldn't know
where they come from.

What are you goin' to be when
you grow up, son?
Bigger, missus.
And were ye born in Dublin, son?
Yea.
What part?
All of me.

Well, didn't the brother call me
in, Maisie, and he says, Oh yer
son's a hopeless case, Mrs.
O'Brien, sure the poor lad
hardly knows who made the
world.
And what did ye say back to him,
luv?
Well, brother, says I, sure 'tis
hardly worth his while to find
out either, for all he'll have of it.

I can't get me young fella to go
to Mass anymore, he says it's
dead boring 'cause he knows the
ending.

What's yer young fella going to
be when he passes his exams?
Oh, from his performance to
date, an old man I'd say.

My young Paddy was sent home from school yesterday 'cause the lad sittin' next to him was smoking.
And why was your lad sent home then?
Well, I think that it was Paddy that set him on fire.

Young Mark got a part in a play. It's a very important part — he has to deliver a letter.
Is that all?
Oh, but it's a registered letter.

I nearly murdered my two young fellas last night, Bridie. There they were playing bridge in me good room.
And, sure what's wrong with that?
Well, one of them was between me two good chairs and the other fella was walking on top of him.

I think Mary's young fella is a bit like that.
A bit like what?
Ye know, a bit of a molly.
Oh no, luv, she says that he's completely bisexual.

And when is she due, Bridie?
Oh, very soon now, luv, she says the babby's been kickin' her all mornin'.
Jaysus, and it hasn't even seen her yet.

. . . and then the husband says to her, I'd like to be present at the birth of the baby. Better for you, says she, if you'd been there at the conception.

Would ye look at that long drink o' water that Sally's young fella turned into.
Oh, I don't know, luv. I'd say that he's improved a bit. I remember him as a babby. Jaysus, he was so ugly that she used to have to hide him out in the back or the postman wouldn't deliver the letters.

**That turkey is after eating me
crisps again, Mary. I'll be
sorry to wring his neck,
though, 'cause I think he was
looking forward to
Christmas.**

Are ye buying a turkey, missus?
Oh, no thanks, luv, sure please
God me husband will be giving
me a goose this Christmas.
Jaysus, I'd say you could do with
one alright, Mam.

**That turkey hasn't a pick on
him, he must have been doing
the Lenten fast.
Ye must have been doing it
yourself, mister, that looks
very much like sackcloth ye'r
wearing.**

Hey, missus, is that turkey for
eating or is it in training to run a
race?

**Hey, missus, one of yer turkeys
is after escaping. Have ye got
yer lasso or will I shoot to
kill?
Would ye ever shoot yerself in
the heart, luv, and drop dead.**

*Missus, did ye kill that turkey
yerself or did it commit
suicide?*

Missus, are ye selling bangers for
Christmas?
Jesus, son, do ye want to have me
arrested? Come back in half an
hour when it's all quiet on the
western front.

**Missus, will ye get goose
pimples if ye touch that
goose?
Oh, ye'r so funny son, one wit
more now and ye'll be a half
wit.**

Will ye sell us some bangers for
Christmas?
I'll tell ye, son, I'll sell ye anything
within reason, and if money is the
reason, I'll sell anything.

Well, Theresa, will ye get your
stockin' filled this Christmas?
Oh, I will, luv, with me bleedin'
leg.

Well, he gave me a Christmas
bonus last night. I was a bit taken
aback, though, 'cause I was
expecting cash.

**Well, I'll tell you, Bridie, if
them carol singers don't stop
singing that Away in a
Manger soon, they'll have me
away in an asylum.**

Hey, young fella, is that ring in yer nose so that we can lead ye around?

Hey, Maisie, what will I have to give ye to get a passion kiss?
An anaesthetic, luv.

Hey, Rosie, I'll say this much for ye, ye bring out the animal in me.
Jaysus, keep away from me, luv, I've always been afraid of mice.

Hey, Maisie, you've a great pair of headlights there.
Well, son, isn't it better than having two flat tyres up front?

I'll tell ye what, Bridie, ye'r just my kind of woman, I go for the mature type.
Jaysus, would ye listen to him. Hold on there a minute, luv, and I'll introduce you to me grandmother.

Now, don't rise me now, mister, ye'd be better off to try a little bit of flattery, sure it might get ye into more interesting places.

. . . and I'll bring ye a nice bunch of flowers, says he. Flowers! says I. Jaysus, I need flowers like a hole in the head and I trying to flog them to earn a living every day of me life. I ask ye.

Well, there was I in the pub, and over he comes and says that he wouldn't insult me by offerin' me a drink.
And what did ye say to that?
Oh, says I, I was always one to swally an insult.

There ye are now, Chrissie, and ye don't look a day older.
No, luv, not since yesterday.

Jaysus, luv, ye look so great today that if ye looked any better I couldn't stand it.

You'd like to speak to somebody with a little authority?

Well, ye'r speaking to the right person, sir, sure haven't I as little authority around here as anybody.

Missus, I have a complaint about those potatoes that I bought off you last week. Eatin' them was like having a few bars of carbolic soap in me mouth.

Well, beggin' yer pardon, sir, they must be still there, from all the bubbles that's coming out of it.

Ye want to see the boss? Well, I'll tell ye, I'm the boss, can't ye see that by the big blue vein swelling up in me forehead.

There he is, buying nothin' again. Jaysus, the only way to get anything outa him would be to use a vacuum cleaner.

Ye want a refund! Merciful hour! Girls, do ye hear this, he wants a refund. Jaysus, luv, you'll be asking me to swop ye something next.

*There's yer oranges, now,
    missus, and have a nice
    holiday.
Pardon?
I said, there's yer oranges
    and have a nice holiday, are
    ye bleedin' deaf?*

Hey, young fella, hands off them
    apples, have ye never read in yer
    catechism about forbidden fruit?
    Well, here it is in person.

I'll give you 5p for an apple,
    missus.
You'll give me a pain in me neck
    if ye don't clear off now, son.
Ah, ye can stick yer oul' apples,
    ye wouldn't be goin' on at me like
    this if I was spending plenty of
    money now, would ye?
Ah no, luv, but ye'r not, are ye?
    Listen, son, clear off now, I've
    enough thorns in me side without
    the addition of a prick like
    yourself.

• FLOWERS •

---

*Missus, will these flowers last
    a long time, then?
Ah, isn't that the six-mark
    question, luv. Sure if any of
    us were cut off in our bloom
    and then put up to our arse in
    water would we hold out very
    long?*

**I believe those flowers are
    beginning to wither a little.
Oh, don't trouble yerself about
    them, missus, sure by this
    afternoon I'll have them
    certified dead.**

Do ye want a loan of me
    handkerchief there, luv?
No, why, missus?
Well, I thought ye might have a
    cold on ye, 'cause it looks like ye'r
    wipin' yer nose on me flowers.

Lovely roses, missus, will ye take a few?

I'll get them on the way back, missus.

Oh, ye'll have to hurry then, 'cause I have here the last rose of summer.

• VEGETABLES •

Do ye want any vegetables, mister?

No.

Ah, go on, sure a nice dose of greens might put ye in good humour.

Ye can't see the vegetables underneath.

Well, there's nothing I can do about that, luv, except to tell ye that there's an opticians up in O'Connell Street.

Hey, missus, them vegetables are stirring about a bit.

That's all right sir, I think they're beginning to breed. It must be the mating season.

Are them swedes, missus?

I'm not sure of their nationality, luv.

If that's all, son, I wish ye'd move on. Thank ye for buying the veg but unfortunately I won't be able to cook them for ye today.

He wants to know have we got any asparagus.

Tell him none, luv, apart from me veins.

Hey, missus, looking at the size of them little potatoes, I'm not surprised there was a famine.

Missus, aren't them sprouts very small.

Sure, maybe they're boy sprouts, son.

Missus, I think I seen them tomatoes moving in their box a while ago.

And wouldn't you be getting restless now, son, if you were lying about in the same box for the past three days?

Any tomatoes today, Sadie?

No, luv, I'm afraid they're as scarce as hobby horse manure.

• PLANTS •

Jaysus, Mary, it'll be like autumn here soon with them bleedin' plants startin' to die on me. I'd better try and give them the kiss of life quick before they fall down at me feet.

Hey, missus, will that plant grow anywhere?
Indeed it will, son, sure 'tis like love-making, you can have it in a bed or up against the wall.

Can ye tell if them is male or female plants, missus?
No, not by looking at them, luv, ye'd have to examine the roots.
Jaysus, it must be very frustrating having yer roots buried in six inches of dirt.

Missus, if I buy that rubber plant will I be able to make me own contraceptives?
Go on with ye, 'tis yerself is the best walking ad for contraception around.

• HENS •

I hear eggs is going up again, missus!
Jaysus, luv, that'll be a bit of a shock to the hens, they must have lost all sense of direction.

Missus, are them eggs fresh?
I only laid the counter, luv.

There seems to be feathers inside this chicken, missus.
Well, that's strange, sir, 'cause they usually grow on the outside.

Isn't it funny, Bridie, that when eggs are cheap the hens seem to lay a lot of them, but when they're dear they don't give as many.

• FRUIT •

Hey, missus, are them bananas
good for a body?
Them's the things, son, to put the
starch back in yer britches.

**I think them bananas is
turning black.
Maybe they're pining for
Africa, luv.**

Missus, if ye eat them bananas will
ye be swinging from the trees
after?
If ye don't clear off outa' here now,
son, you'll be swinging from a
rope.

---

*Aren't them bananas still a bit
green, missus?
Oh, sure, they're only newly in
this mornin', luv. A special
delivery by Tarzan from the
Amazon and handpicked by
the man himself.*

. . . and could I put these into a
fresh fruit salad now?
With every respect, missus, as long
as ye buy them ye can bounce
them off the ceiling after, for all I
care.

**Hey, Bridie, I think that
banana is after moving.
Jaysus, luv, quick, get a stick
and kill it.**

Enjoy those mushrooms now, luv,
but if I were you I wouldn't eat
the one with the little door and
the chimney.

Well, mister, are ye goin' to buy
them vegetables or do you have to
ask yer wife for your opinion?

Missus, them oranges are very
dried up and shrivelled looking.
Well, listen, if you had to come all
the way from South Africa
wouldn't ye run outa' juice
yerself?

Yes, luv, three oranges — I heard
ye, I'm not deaf, but if ye keep up
that shouting at me, I will be in
the next five minutes.

There's five of them oranges for
50p, missus.
I'll tell ye what, I'll give ye 20p for
three.
I'll take it, luv, I suppose at this
hour of the evening it's better
than a kick in the arse.

Hey, missus, are ye selling them
oranges?
No, luv, I'm going to give them
their civil rights and liberate them
this afternoon.

It's no use stroking those
oranges, luv, I've tamed them
meself already.

Missus, do ye sell fruit juice?
No, luv, but looking at these
oranges all day I feel I could piss
it for ye.

**Well, I think I'll take a dozen of
those blood oranges.
I'm glad ye made up yer mind
at last, missus, 'cause I was
afraid that they were going to
start to haemorrhage.**

Hey, missus, I'm just after finding
a long maggot in this apple I'm
eating.
Well, wouldn't it be worse now,
son, if you had found half a
maggot?

---

*Tell me, missus, have you
worked down here all your
life?*
No, son, not yet.

Would ye like something to eat,
mister, while ye'r deciding what
to buy?

**Jaysus, luv, there's no one
buying grapes at all this week.
Maybe they got rid of all the
patients up in the Rotunda.**

Have you got pigs feet, missus?
No, luv, it's just these new shoes I'm
wearin'.

Hey, missus, can I have a leek?
I'd love a leak meself, sir, but I
have to stay at this stall for
another half an hour.

**Missus, is there a toilet around
here?
Anywhere you like at all
between here and Capel
Street.**

Missus, is Fenian Street around
here?
Well, it's around here somewhere,
luv, but I think you'd be better
off startin' lookin' from
somewhere else.

**. . . Well, the cheek of that
bitch, she said that I must be
selling stuff that the bin men
refused to take away. But I
can tell ye, luv, I hit her so
hard, I was dug outa her.**

Mary, isn't it strange, like, with all them cars not moving at all, that they call it the rush hour?

Would ye look at yer wan, she's running so fast after that bus, that her legs will catch fire.

Isn't it funny — that bus home always seems to go faster when ye'r after it than when ye'r on it.

I've never seen the street so busy, Bridie, with all the coming and going down here this morning it's like a cowboy film.

Knocked down by a car he was on his way home from the pub. Oh, his missus is in a terrible state. I'll tell you something, it wasn't an act of God but an act of Guinness.

Look at that now, the poor man after breaking a leg and he after comin' up on the pools too last week. Well, there ye are now, there's no windfall without a downfall.

Mary rang her at four o'clock the other mornin' and she fast asleep.
Did she mind?
No, not really, sure, she had to get up to answer the phone anyway.

There goes the burglar alarm in that place again. Wouldn't ye think the owners would stay in sometime and be there to turn it off.

Ye know, luv, I think that young wan goes around sucking them lollipops just to excite the oul' fellas.

Well, that girl was born lucky. I can remember her as a babby on her first day out, sure when she first saw the sun wasn't it shinin'?

Bernie said that they're so strict in that factory, even if you're absent that ye have to go and mark absent in the book.

Isn't it strange with these forms, Bridie, that ye always have to put yer second name down first, at the start.

Would I want a drink? Is that what ye'r after askin' me? Would a duck swim?

Ye know, Mary, I read
somewhere that we only use
a third of our brain.
Jaysus, luv, I wonder what
happens to the other third?

Ye know, I think I'll take up
that meditation thing this
winter. Wouldn't it be better,
now, than sittin' around and
doing nothing?

I'll tell you, Bridie, the only
thing I'd expect on a silver
platter is tarnish.

---

*Standing here, luv, sure
you'd hardly notice the
transition between life and
death.*

• FASHION •

Isn't that a nice dress that
Jacinta is wearing today?
'Tis, luv, it'll be even nicer
when it's finished.
Ah it's not bad.
No, especially when ye consider
that it was on their front winda
last week.

Chrissie, come here a minute
and look at the figure on this
wan.
Merciful hour! The last time I
saw a figure like that, the owner
was being milked.

Would ye look, talk about
mutton dressed up as lamb,
in that skirt at her age.
Wouldn't ye think she'd
catch herself on.
I'll tell ye what, luv, if she
doesn't stop wearing them
short skirts, she'll bring on
the change of life quicker.

Mary's just back from the
hairdresser. Would ye look at
her perm. I think I can see the
singe marks on her neck.

Hey, Paddy, ye'r all dolled up
today, ye'r the real minstrel boy
now in yer jacket green. Ye'r
not thinking now of going into
the St Patrick's Day parade be
any chance?

Hey, Paddy, I wouldn't
bother growing that beard if
I were you. Do the decent
thing and give yerself up to
the police.

Look at her coat, Bridie, is it an
eiderdown or what?
Well, all I can say, luv, is it's
either that or a patchwork quilt.
The poor woman must think
that she's still in bed.

Isn't he a very smart dresser.
Oh, very smart, the real Mickey dazzler. Ye
know, I heard he used to dress off the peg
until the neighbours decided to take in their
washin'.

Mother of God, with those earrings and that war paint for make-up wouldn't ye swear that the Last of the Mohicans had come to Moore Street.

Would ye look at the two red cheeks of her. Oh, I'd say the Messenger cover has been dipped in that house.

Her weddin' dress was lovely, Mary, the skirt was long and pleated with a simple bodice and it fell to her ankles. She had a bouquet of red carnations and a trailer.

I notice you're not sittin' down at all today, Theresa. No, luv, me new jeans won't bend.

You know, Mary, I think that them punk fellas with their chains and haircuts and filthy clothes are not happy until someone looks at them and gets sick.

Missus, are them lobsters
fresh?
No, sir, I have to wind them
all up every morning.

Missus, I think that lobster has
lost a claw.
Jaysus, you're right, luv, he
must have been in a fight.
Well, I think I'd better have
that other one then, he must
have been the winner.

Have you got any crabs,
missus?
I don't know, luv, I didn't look
this morning.

**Did ye see the way that
crab's been moving about all
day, Bridie? Jaysus, I think
he must have got the side
effects from something he
ate.**

I'd be careful now, luv, if you
keep on sniffin' that whitenin'
you might get addicted.

That's a very small whitenin',
missus.
What do you expect for 10p,
luv, the great white whale?

I don't know whether I'll take
two of these or one of those.
Missus, if ye don't hurry on
and decide, the fish will put
their coats on and go home.

Hey, missus, are them
prawns pure, genuine Dublin
Bay's?
Listen, luv, I only buy the
fish, I don't swim around
with them, as well.

That one there looks like a
jellyfish, missus.
Yes, luv, but it hasn't its mind
made up yet. It's just about to
set now.

**How much are them kippers,
missus?**
50p for three, luv.
Will ye give us two for 20p?
Jaysus, luv, I have to buy
them fish meself ye know,
they don't give themselves
up.

Missus, that one there looks a
bit different from the rest.
How's that?
Oh, I'd keep away from him,
luv, he's dangerous — that's
Jack the Kipper, ye know.

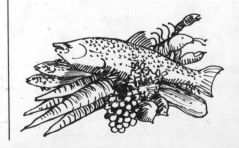

Missus, them fish is very small,
there isn't a pick on them.
And what do ye expect, luv,
feathers?

**Them fish is still alive and
flappin' about.
Oh, don't mind them, son,
they're auditioning for a
part in Moby Dick.**

Do ye have a glass bowl to go
with them fish?
A glass bowl? What do ye want
that for son?
Well, missus, they're so small
they're hardly worth eating, sure
I'd be better off looking at
them.

**Are them eels, missus? God,
I don't like the look of them.
Well, I don't expect ye to
love and cherish them,
missus, just take 'em home
and shove 'em on a pan.**

Are ye sure they're all right
now?
Well, I couldn't really say, son;
maybe it's either sea sickness or
travel sickness that's up with
them.

Missus, sure there's no need to
say 'fresh fish today'. When ye'r
selling them today now we all
presume they're fresh.
Listen, luv, if youse don't clear
off with yer today, I won't be
long drivin' ye into the middle
of next week.

Now, missus, I hope you're not
selling any red herrings there.
No, luv, they're all off colour
today.

---

*Hey, missus, I don't like the
smell of them mackerel.
Listen, luv, it's fish I'm
sellin', not daffodils; what
do ye want them to smell
like? Woolworth's perfume?*

Oh, he says that he never turned to drink but that it turned to him.
I wouldn't mind that fella, luv, sure he was born in a glass.

Would ye look at him now, luv,
staggering around and he not
able to put a leg under him.
Oh, indeed, and I believe that
his eyes are so bad that he keeps
running into pubs.

Look at that fella there, Bridie,
not able to put a leg under him,
leaning up against the wall.
Yes, luv, that's plastered as
well.

**Well, if he's not drunk he
should be on the stage
because his act is fantastic.**

Well, I'd like me job askin' that
fella to give up the drink for
Lent, sure he'd lick it off a sore
leg all the year round.
Ah sure, luv, what would ye
expect from a pig, but a grunt.

Would ye look at long-nose
Pinocchio, he told me this
morning that his throat is
terrible sore.
I'm not surprised, luv, with all
that gargle goin' down it.
Jaysus, he'd need sluice gates.

**Oh, I hear he's giving up the
drink. Well fancy that, I'd
say, now, that his lips will
start to put on weight for
the lack of exercise.**

Here's me oul' fella now,
Maisie, after being in the pub
all day. Look at him now, not
able to put a leg under him.
Oh indeed, luv, he's the real
stupor man. There he is
bellowin' like a loudspeaker and
he tryin' to pull up the parkin'
meters.
Jaysus, luv, why did I ever marry
six foot of bad luck?

opposite

Jaysus, luv, he must be walking
like that so as not to spill any of
it. Isn't he the real methylated
martyr now?

Ye'r full of whiskey, says I. Oh, not quite full yet, says he. Ye know, Maisie, they're not happy 'till they can make a meal out of it.

No, luv, I'm not drunk. As Brendan would say, I'm ebbin and flowin' — sure aren't the Guinness family very good to us and haven't we to be good to Guinness as well.

A hangover! Course I have a hangover, sure what's a hangover? As Brendan Behan said, A hangover for me is when the brew of the night meets the dawn of the day.

And does Tommy drink, Bridie?
Oh, like a fish, luv, but it's a pity they don't drink the same stuff.

Oh, yer man's a hard drinker, luv.
Well, I'm surprised to hear that, luv, because after all this time, I'd have thought he'd have found it easy.

Jaysus, Mick, there's eatin' and drinking' in that pint, sure you could take yer knife and fork to it.

His only drink problem is that he doesn't have the money to pay for it.

If I was you, luv, I'd keep away from that fella. He's got a one track mind, and it's a dirt track. With him it's all wine, women and so long.

I'd get all I could outa him now, luv, because when he's gone, you won't be able to pawn the romance.

Now, I'm not saying he's oversexed, Mary, but I'd watch the drawers on me dresser when he's around.

And, luv, I wouldn't get into that oul' Morris Minor of his, sure it's like riding around in a teapot.

Did you know him well, Bridie? Well, I'll tell you, luv, I knew him well enough to borrow from but not well enough to lend to.

I must ask Jimmy to try and fix me barra with that pliers. I wouldn't bother if I were you, luv, sure he's useless, a pliers to him would be like a cross to a vampire.

Hey, Billy, yer flies are open. Careful now, luv, or yer brains will get cold.

Hey, Billy, if I were you, I'd watch the exhaust fumes from that horse and cart.

And, Jacinta, don't let him pull the wool over yer eyes tonight, keep yer jumper on.

Here, son, hold out yer left hand here for this. No son, gimme yer other left hand.

That wan says she knows the days that she can do her washing from looking at her husband in the morning. If it's lying to the right she says it'll be a fine day, but if it's lying to the left rain is on the way. And what if it's standing up in the middle? Sure, Jaysus, luv, who'd want to do anything on a day like that?

Be careful that ye don't swally that packet of seeds, luv, or yer arse might be in bloom.

Hush, Paddy, keep yer voice
down, here's that fella with
the transparent ears again.

Are ye still suffering from
the rheumatism, Maisie?
No, luv, I'm beginning to
enjoy it now.

You know, Bridie, standing up all
day is great for me piles.

Jaysus, luv, don't work too hard.
If ye faint here standing up
you'll collapse on to the ground.

**Oh, Mary, me varacus veins
is killin' me today. I have
three yards of knotted rope
inside me legs.**

It's the standing all day that's
giving me the flat feet. Maybe I
should take the bicycle pump to
them.

**Now, luv, on account of the
standing all day you should
take deep breaths. Listen,
take a deep breath from
your stomach, keep it in as
long as possible and then
expire slowly.**

Ye know, luv, lately I've been
feeling dog tired and listless,
and if I stand up suddenly I get
dizzy.
Me daughter says she has to
smoke fifty to feel like that.

I'd watch that cough if I were
her. The last person I heard
coughin' like that is up in
Glasnevin.

**I'll tell ye, Maisie, since I
started smoking again me
lungbago has come back with
a vengeance.**

Jaysus, after givin' up the
smokin' I don't know now what
to do with me hands.

Oh, I'm feeling dreadful, luv, I
was very bilious all night and
I've a very bad head this
morning, but sure maybe I'll
shake it off during the day.

Oh, me nerves, and the mental
cruelty of it! I've been under
me doctor's sedatives now for a
week.

I tell ye, Bridie, I've taken so
many tablets for me nerves this
morning that ye could sell me
off there now as one of them
vegetables and I wouldn't know
the difference.

Ye should go and have yer nose seen to. I heard they're doing cut price operations below in Jervis Street.

Is the hearing still bad with you, Katie? You know you could have an operation to improve that.
Well, I think, luv, that at eighty-eight years of age, now, I've heard enough.

I've heard young Patricia isn't too well, May?
Oh, I don't think it's too bad, luv. She'll probably be up and sleepin' around in no time.

No, she says that she's not feelin' well — that she's either comin' down with a cold or else she's expectin'.
Well, I wonder now who could have given her a cold.

The poor woman, may I be stiffened if I'm telling a lie. I was giving her the hint, discreetly like, about hygiene when she says to me, Oh I wouldn't use that stuff at all, says she, sure I'll stick to the powder that me mother always used and that's Mrs. Cullens.

Complain, complain, ye never heard the like of it. If it's not her feet it's her back. She asked me this morning, an' I up to me eyes, what would she take for her migraine.
What did ye say to her?
You're too common to have migraine, says I. Why don't ye just take yerself now with a pinch of salt?

Well, she says she has to be x-rayed tomorrow at Jervis Street.
I'll tell ye what, luv, if I was that doctor I'd ultra violate.

Hey, Bridie, I think I'm putting on far too much weight. Standing around here ye get no exercise.
Indeed ye'r not, luv. Sure, don't we love every acre of ye!

Jaysus, me kidney stone is acting up again today. It's cuttin' thru me at the minute. I'll tell ye, now, if I had a penknife I'd try and get it out meself.

I'm seeing Dr Flynn tonight, Annie.
Jaysus, luv, I've heard that fella couldn't cure a ham.

Oh, I couldn't go to that doctor, Mary, lying down on a couch for an hour and then gettin' a bill for it afterwards — Jaysus!

I hear her young fella is suffering from consumption.
Oh, I thought it was TB, luv.

I don't think young Jacinta is looking her best today, Mary. The fellas is startin' to count their change.

Jacinta, luv, is that jaundice ye have or did ye buy some make-up over in Woolworths?

Jaysus, if that fella put on a clean pair of socks sure his shoes wouldn't fit him.

Jimmy Byrne strong and well built! Ye must be joking, luv, the only mussels that fella has are the ones he fecked off me stall last Monda.

I'd love to be a man, Maisie, then I wouldn't have to kiss someone who had'nt washed or shaved for three days.

Ye know, Bridie, every time we breathe a person dies. Maybe we should use a good mouthwash, luv.

Jaysus, Paddy, keep away from that barber. Sure, going to him is like having a shave with a tin can.

• INSULTS AND THREATS •

Hey, missus, I caught ye this time, and don't tell me that orange is after jumping into yer bag.

I'm tellin' ye, if I catch ye near them oranges again I'll break yer snot. Clear off, ye hoor's melt.

Now, I'm warnin' ye, clear off. I was beginning to enjoy the air around here until you arrived. Listen, if ye'r going somewhere, I'd arrive there early.

Missus, ye'r starting to foam at the mouth. I think ye have the rabies. I'd better move off now before ye start to bite me.

Go on with ye, don't you look at me in that tone of voice — with yer plucked eyebrows and bad teeth. Jaysus, ye should be at a bullfight, in the ring.

Off with ye now, ye bockedy-arsed oul' bitch, 'tis up in the azoo lookin' out at the people ye should be.

Now listen here, missus, you keep yer nose outa this unless ye want it at the back of yer face.

Hey oul' wan, give us a loan of your face to stop a dog fight.

Go on with ye, even if your parents had got married you'd still have been a bastard.

Missus, did ye ever think of sellin' yer face as a prune?

That bitch wouldn't get a job making beds in a brothel.

Go on with ye and yer oul' face that would stop a clock.
Well, even a stopped clock is right twice a day, luv, which is more than can ever be said for yourself.

Oh, ye can hit that fella all right, mister, he's no relation of mine.

Careful now, or you might wake up with a crowd around ye.

Hey, mister, what are ye ejaculating out of ye now?

Poor, is it, son? Jaysus, ye'r so fuckin' poor, that ye couldn't keep a prostitute.

Now listen here, if you don't clear off I'll hit you so many times that you'll think you're surrounded.

Ye never seen the like of it. They were worse than cavemen from Kimmage — and ye know they eat their children out there.

I'm tellin' ye, Josie, ye'r well able for that bitch. Jaysus, ye went through her for a shortcut. You've a tongue on ye like a razor.
Well, luv, she'll get more than a a close shave by the time I'm finished with her.

Well, if ye heard the language of him! Jaysus, if me mother was still alive she'd turn in her grave.

Luv, I never forget a face but in your case I'm prepared to make an exception.

• LAW •

No, Garda, I'm not illegal, I have me licence. Do ye want to play with that now instead of playing with yer handcuffs?

So, she was brought up to court? Indeed she was, luv. Didn't she go for the husband with the knife and give him a fair going over. However, she told the justice that it was he who ran into her knife.
What did he say to that?
He said that he was a bit surprised that her oul' fella ran into it ten times.

Mary, have you ever been picked up by the fuzz?
No, luv, but I'd say it hurts.

opposite

Ye know, Masie, yer man got off the shop lifting for absence of mind.
Jaysus, they should have mentioned absence of body as well.
Yea, he's not the full shilling, is he?

• LOVE AND MARRIAGE •

Oh, complain, complain. Sure I can't satisfy my fella at all. That's a very stale cake, says he last night at the tea. Oh, sorry, sorry, says I, I must have used an old recipe by mistake.

Well, luv, did ye give him the ten oysters before going to bed to get him goin' like I told ye?
Indeed I did, luv, but I think that only five of them worked.

. . . and then! he suggests that we do it doggie style.
Well, I hope ye put ye'r paw down, luv?

Do ye know the facts of life at all? says he to me. Listen, luv, says I, I bleedin' know the facts of life, but I don't like them.

Will ye still love him when he's no longer able to satisfy ye in bed, Josie?
Oh, I do, luv, I do.

I'll tell ye, Bridie, I'm totally against divorce. Why should anyone get off what I've had to suffer for the last twenty years?
Well, I'll tell ye one thing - if ye had killed him on the honeymoon, ye'd be out be now.

Isn't it terrible all the same, luv,
when ye start to put on a few
years ye'r left to yerself. I
remember well the time when
my fella couldn't wait for me to
take off me stockings. Jaysus,
now I have time to knit a pair.

Josie, when ye got married were
ye virgo intacta?
Jaysus, I don't know, luv, maybe
me mother might remember.

That Katie and her husband
haven't spoken now for a
month.
Oh, I don't think he wants to
interrupt her.

The poor woman says that she
can't suffer any more of it, that
she's going to see the priest and
look for a separation.
Well, I'll tell ye, luv, if it was my
husband, the separation he'd get
is that I'd fuckin' separate his
head from his shoulders.

**So, she's no longer married
and unhappy then?**
**No, luv, now she's separated
and grateful.**

And does he snore in his sleep,
luv?
Oh, I don't know yet. Sure we've
only been married three days.

But of course she has to stay
with him, luv. Didn't she wed
him for life? Pity it was after,
though, that she found out he
didn't have any.

Well, she told me that he's a
fornicator.
What's that?
I'm not sure, now, but I think
that he'll be dead in a few years.
Well, at least she'll have him
lookin' down on her then.
I'd say, luv, in his position
he'd be more likely to be lookin'
up.

**Mary says that what with the
family breakin' up, and
herself breakin' down, that
there will be none of them
there at all in a month's
time.**

She told me that she was mad to
marry him.
Well, I don't know, luv, I'd say
he was just as daft to propose.

**Well, ye know, Biddy I had a
feeling that that marriage
wouldn't last. Ye know when
she showed me how the
photos of the weddin' had
turned out I had a sort of
premonition.**

Maisie, I heard young Noreen
was trying to get out of the
engagement, how did she get
on?
Oh, she got out of it all right,
luv, she married the ghet.

And Lizzie says now that she'll only let him have his way with her during the safe period — that's when her husband is away.

How are ye, Billy? Ye'r up early this mornin'. Where's the missus?
Oh, me sleeping bag? She won't be up till noon.

He says his wife is an angel.
Jaysus, he's lucky. I didn't know she was dead yet.

. . . and she says to make sure that he doesn't leave her standin' at the altar that she's going to wheel him to church in the barra.

Well, Paddy says that the missus is great at doin' bird imitations, that she watches him like a hawk.

I don't think that I'll be invited to that weddin', Rosie.
Well, I don't know, luv, but maybe they'd like the honour of your present anyway.

Oh, it must be great now
when ye'r married, Angela?
Oh, it's great, luv, whether
ye'r married or not.

God, I haven't seen her for an age, and look at the state of her now. Is that a pilla she has up her skirt or did she forget to put on her corset?

Oh, she's put on a bit all right, luv. Keep out of her way, now, or she might fall on ye.

Would ye look at her, Bridie, the size of her. She has so many chins that she's like a sliced pan.

Jaysus, I'd put handles on the cups of that bra if I were her, it might be easier to stand up.

Now, I won't say she's fat, but whenever she gets on a weighing machine out comes a card saying come back when you're alone.

No, I'm not saying she has a bad figure but I've seen better legs on a table.

That wan, wouldn't ye think she'd buy something and try and fatten up that husband of hers.

Oh, she says it's his nature to be thin, that he was born that way.

And, luv, he'll die that way livin' with her.

Hey, Maisie, it doesn't look as if she's buying much for the husband's tea tonight.

Oh, the poor man. Ye know, I saw him in Harold's Cross last week and I mistook him for one of the greyhounds.

Oh no, luv, that family never see meat. She brings them vegetables from me all the time. Sure if one of them saw a butcher's shop wouldn't they think there had been an accident.

I believe her husband has finally got work.

Yea, I heard he's selling furniture and they say they're down now to the bed.

And she says the husband gets meat every day.

Indeed! Well so do the lions in the azoo.

What's she buying all that cabbage every day for I wonder?

Oh, I heard she gives it to them in sandwiches.

Jaysus, do ye see the big flowery hat on that wan, isn't she the real Mary Hick. Well, all I can say is she'd better keep away from Glasnevin or they might mistake if for a wreath.

Oh, she's so full of herself now there's no talkin' to her. She told me that she'd been specially selected to examine a set of encyclopedias on a free home trial.
Jaysus, luv, they'll probably use them for toilet paper.
Well, I suppose it'll be a change for them havin' some.

. . . and where's she getting the money for them things at all?
Oh, she's buying them on the never-never, luv. Ye know, if it wasn't for Cavendishes and the bit of tick at the corner shop that wan could neither eat nor sit.

Here's ye'r wan again, all bottom and no brains.

Look at that wan there, drippin' with glamour and a tan on her like a crisp with legs.

There she is now, Sadie, out in her figure. And would you say that that figure's all her own?
I don't know, luv, but I'd say there might be more in her belly than ever went in through her mouth.

Here she is now, with her face lift. Well luv, it might be higher up, but it's just as ugly.

But I hear yer wan's a very good cook, Mary.
Jaysus, luv, I'd say the only thing that wan knows about cookin' is how to bring her oul fella to the boil.

Mary, how many husbands has that wan had?
You mean apart from her own?

Well, did ye hear her? Wouldn't she talk the teeth off a saw, and the airs and graces — well I never. I nearly dropped dead when she mentioned the jacuzzi. Between you and me, I'd say the nearest that wan ever got to a jacuzzi was a fart in the bath.

Now she's wondering whether she'll stay on butter or change to margarine. Wouldn't she give you the sick. I'll tell ye, it's far from either she was reared. Jaysus, they were lucky if they saw a bit of lard once a month.

She's buying all around her — I don't know where they're gettin' the money. I can remember a time when they were so badly off they thought knives and forks were jewellery.

I believe she's getting very religious, luv. She was seen over in Adam and Eve's on her knees, praying.
Praying? On her knees? Well, I suppose in that position praying would be a brand new experience for her.

She says she has temporary amnesia and she can't seem to remember things.
Well, the poor girl. But sure even before her loss of memory, she kept forgettin' who her husband was.

Well, luv, I hear that at this stage everyone's been up on her apart from the 46A!

Would ye look at her. Well, at least now that she's expectin' it balances up the hunch on her back.

I will say something for that poor girl, Bridie, she may not look much but she speaks beautifully.
Oh, indeed she does, luv. It's a pity, though, that she says nothing.

That poor woman is so secretive.
Secretive? If you gave her a needle, wouldn't she build a haystack around it.

Jewellery! Jewellery me arse! That's her rosary beads round her neck that she's trying to pass off as a necklace.

Would ye look at the legs on her. Jaysus, they're like spaghetti on drugs.

She says she saw a mouse in her larder last night.
Oh, that shouldn't bother her. It'll probably starve to death.

Now, I'm not saying they're poor, luv, but I believe she used to try and polish the window with the kitten.

Her new house out in Kimmage is lovely, Bridie. It's a little one-storey house, that's whitewashed yella, and they can sleep upstairs.

Poor! I believe that when something falls off the table in that house that the children are on the floor before it hits the ground.

I believe that in the oul' tenement they're in the rain comes down the walls like water.

They say yer man's very
intelligent.
Intelligent! Jaysus, that fella has a
mind like cold tripe.

---

*I've been told, Bridie, that it's
so tough down there that the
rent man stands at the top
of the street, shouts out 'any
rent' and then runs.*

Mary, look at that huge big wan
with the little oul fella.
Oh, he must be her lunch, luv.

**Hey, mister, why did ye get
the dog?**
Oh, I got it for the wife.
**Jaysus, ye made a good
bargain there.**

Well, all I can say is, I don't
know what he wants a dog for,
with that bitch of a wife with
him. That wan shouldn't be let
out without a lead.

Would ye look at that fella with
all the scratches on his face.
Oh, I think he's learning to eat
with a fork.

**Paddy told me once it often
crossed his mind to go into
the army.**
**Crossed his mind! That's a
good one — there's one thing
sure, it didn't have a long
journey.**

Well, ye know, Mary, I'll give
that fella credit for one thing —
he always pays cash.

Bridie, would ye look. There
go the snot sisters again with
their noses in the air.
The poor girls. I'll tell ye,
Mary, what their trouble is now
— they're both suffering from
virginity.

**Did ye hear what Paddy
Kavanagh said to yer man?
He said, I know you have a
mouth in ye, sure how could
I miss it and it swinging
between your two ears like a
skipping rope?**

Where's yer husband, Bridie? I haven't seen him for the last few days.

Well, ye've heard of a sit-down strike, luv, but my fella's on a lie-down strike at home in bed.

Oh, he's not feeling the best at all. He says that when he gets up in the morning and looks in the mirror that he gets sick all over the place.

Well, I'll say this much for him, his eyesight must be all right.

My fella says that after a shave in the morning, he feels ten years younger.

Jaysus, I wish my Jack would shave last thing at night, then.

Have ye seen my fella, Maisie? Here a minute ago and now after scarperin' off. Jaysus, the scarlet pimpernel is only trottin' after that fella.

My fella's as unpredictable as a grapefruit's squirt.

Jaysus, only for that wheelbarra, luv, he'd never get up and walk on his hind legs.

I wouldn't clean that barra if I were him, it's only the muck that's holding it together.

Me husband can't stand up for himself at all, he'd be massacred in a fight.

But doesn't he train as a boxer? I thought I seen him shadow boxing once.

Oh, certainly, but the shadow wins every time.

When he's bringing flowers for no reason you can be sure there's a reason.

There's no give and take with men.

Oh, I know the feeling, luv. They do all the givin' and you have to do all the takin'.

Oh, indeed, and ye know, luv, once ye've got it, ye've had it.

Ye know, Mary, I think really that the best sex is before sex.

Are ye glad to have your Harry back with ye, luv?

Oh, sure, he's as welcome around me stall as the flies in May.

He's like a blister, luv, he
always appears after the
work is done.

Her husband was sentenced to
life? Well, poor man, sure
life is a very long time.
Indeed it is, but it's not half as
long as death.
Well, I suppose there's one
consolation, luv, at least
she'll know now where he's
spending the night.

Ye weren't here yesterday at all,
Annie.
No, luv, I was at home with
Harry trying to heal the sick.
But with his hangover I might
as well have been trying to raise
the dead.

• PASS-REMARKABLE •

There he is, with his pioneer pin
and the little gold ring for the
Irish. Isn't it strange now, luv,
how many people have been
making a livin' out of a dead
language for so long.

**Oh, sure he's the real
Irishman — a government
job, a house in Foxrock and
a Cork accent.**

Would ye look at that young wan
and the figure on her. She's no
oil paintin', I'm afraid.
Look she's after buying a big
bottle of perfume.
Jaysus, luv, she'd need more than
than behind her ears to get a
fella.

**Oh, a right cur. Didn't he
vomit in the church into the
box marked For the Sick.**

He's still a bachelor, fancy that.
Well, I suppose it's better to be
a bachelor than a bachelor's son
as they say.

No, he's not up in the Dáil,
Maisie, I said he was a member
of Dole Eireann.

So, you've never been up to the
Dáil, Bridie?
No, luv, but I've heard there
isn't much difference between it
and Glasnevin cemetery.

I'd love to be like that wan over there, Bridie, plenty of money, nothin' to do, and all day to do it.
Oh, I don't know, luv, I've heard she's under a lot a strain.
Indeed, it must be terrible having to get up in the morning to dress yourself.

What did that fella with the ten children want now, Bridie?
Oh, more lettuce — four heads.
Jaysus, he must eat like a rabbit as well.

Well, hasn't he come up in the world, luv. It must be a great change for him to be reading a newspaper instead of eating his dinner offa it.

Look at them road workers, Mary, they have no shovels today. Jaysus, they'll have to lean on one another.

Angela, would ye look at that farmer. He must be up for the day.
Oh, over from the west, I'd say, where the men are men, and the sheep are nervous.

Hey, Mary, here's that oul' know-all teacher again. Now, isn't a little learning a dangerous thing?
Indeed, luv, and sure a great deal of knowledge must be fatal.

• PLEASURES OF LIFE •

And can anyone get into that club, Eileen?
Oh yes, luv, it's for ladies and gentlemen regardless of sex.

Do ye see the way they're dancing now with their shaking and twisting and cavorting. Jaysus, if the dog started that lark you'd take him to the vet to be put down.

We had a terrible meal last night in that Chinese place. As well as the dreadful food, we had sweet and sour waiters, and you know you can't get into the place without a reservation, just like a bleedin' Red Indian.

At the pictures last night this fella grabs me and then, all apologies, says he's looking for his seat. Well, you'd better leave mine alone, says I.

I'm going out again tonight. So, I'm going to leave me clothes into the cleaners first, then I'm goin' up Grafton Street to have a good time for the afternoon to prepare meself for later on.

I had to slap his face three times during the evening.
Why? What did he do?
Nothing, luv, I slapped him to see if he was awake.

And what age is Biddy now, Angela?

Eighty-eight, luv, and she still goes out and enjoys herself. But she won't set foot in one of them old folk's clubs.

Why's that?

Oh, she says she doesn't want to have to dance with all those oul' fellas.

• HOLIDAYS •

Were you away at all this year, Mary?

Oh, yea, we went to Teneriffe.

Where's that?

Jaysus, I don't know, luv, we flew.

Did Catherine enjoy her holiday in Greece?

Oh she did, luv. She said that the days were historical but that the nights were hysterical.

Did you have a nice holiday, Josie?

Oh, lovely. We had a choice of hotel room with either a bath or shower.

What's the difference?

Well, luv, with a shower you have to stand up.

What was yer flight like to Corfu, Noelle?

Have you ever been in a plane yourself, luv?

Yea, once.

Well, it was just like tha'.

• PREGNANCY •

You're not serious, luv, she's going to have a child by yer man from Cavendishes, the furniture shop?

That's it, luv, that's the truth. He gave her a free sample and then off with him.

Well, Maisie told me that she's havin' no more, that she's going to practise birth control.

Jaysus, luv, her best birth control would be to leave the lights on.

So Lizzie tells you now that she's not havin' any more babies?

Well, that's a relief. She must have found out at last what was causin' them.

Josie told me that she was going to have the coil inserted.

Jesus, luv, with her that's like locking the stable door after the horse has bolted.

Well? What about Rose and Charlie's babby? Is it a boy or a child?

A boy!

And what weight?

Four pounds, six ounces!

Jaysus, luv, Charlie hardly got his bait back.

Are they pleased that the babby's on the way now?
Oh, they're so pleased now, luv, that they're plannin' to get married.

I hear her parents are goin' with them on the honeymoon.
And does she mind?
Oh no, sure she says it'll be great havin' someone to mind the child.

Sure how could that wan be expectin' and the husband in prison for the past few years?
Well, luv, that's now what I'd call a grudge situation. Someone must have had it in for him while he was away.

Well, she's had six up to now, but I've heard that she won't be havin' any more.
And why's that?
Because her lodger's been moved down to Cork.

Joan's new baby is a bit on the small side. It only weighed four pounds.
Well, I suppose that's not bad when you consider they've only been going out a short time.

Well, there ye are now, when two's company three's the result. She'll have to answer 'I did' now instead of 'I do' at the weddin'.

Look at the wan, in the family way again. Jaysus, if ye shake hands with her she gets pregnant.

Up the pole and she only goin' out with him for three weeks.
Ah, well, as they say, practice makes pregnant.
And did she tell him about the child on the way?
No, luv, I don't think she knows him that well.

And is she happy with the triplets?
Oh, delighted, luv. And ye know, she says that this only happened once in thirty thousand times.
Jaysus, luv, beats me how she finds time to do the housework.

Bridie, have ye heard of them fantasy pregnancies when ye bloat up and there's nothing there at all? Well, luv, I think I have it the other way round.

I was in the pub last night with Rosie and I says to her, Are ye havin' another, Rosie? No, she says, it's just the way me coat's buttoned.

Bridie, what do you think of all these new contraceptives?
Well, I'll tell you what, Mary, I'm staying on the pill 'cause I can't swally the coil.

Ye know, Bridie, there'd be no need for ye to go on contradictives if yer husband had crystal balls 'cause you'd be able to see it coming then.

Jaysus, Maisie, when we were at school there was none of that sex education stuff, sure all we had to look forward to was the break.

Well, I'm surprised to hear that the line is off. I thought they were gettin' on fine together.
Indeed they were, luv. Sure they both liked all the same things — music, films, parties. 'Twas a pity, though, that they didn't like each other.

Oh, he's a very shy lad. Sure he didn't even want the light on when we were having a bit of a coort. I'd rather do it from memory, says he.

So, they're not going to get married after all? I thought he was going to give her everlasting love and affection!
So he was, luv, but it seems she only needed it for a few nights.

Well, ye see, he told her that he followed the medical profession.
So, why did she break it off?
Well, it turned out he was an undertaker.

Mary, I hear the line is off between John and Theresa.
Oh, I think he bit off more than he could chew there, luv. His eyes were bigger than his balls.
Yea, and I told him about her over and over again. But sure I might as well be throwin' apples into an orchard.

Katie told me that Mickey's drivin' her out now every Sunday.
Well, fancy that. I wonder, now, does she ever manage to get into the front seat at all?

Jaysus, Bridie, that oul' fella of seventy is out with a different young wan every night.
Yea, he must have his mind made up that since he can't take it with him he's going to wear it out.

Joe says he's goin' to go out with Marion because he's interested in her breeding.
The cur, does he want her at it straight away?

Ye tell me, now, that she has given up goin' out with that fella?
So she says. She says he was no fun at all — that she'd have more company goin' out with her umbrella.

I heard that them two are getting engaged. It seems he asked for her hand last night.
Well, isn't that strange, now, that he should end up by wanting her hand, and he after having every other part of her first.

Oh, them two are finished. She invited him to come into her heart but I believe he took a wrong direction.

Isn't that fella gorgeous! He's so well built that even if the GPO fell on him he wouldn't splinter.

You were very late for work this afternoon, Mary.
Yea, the fella that was folleying me was walking very slow.

I never ran after a man in me life. I might have walked a bit faster, but I never ran.

Oh, I believe he's a grand lad, he doesn't drink, smoke or interfere with her in any way.
Jaysus, luv, does he make his own dresses as well?

Mother of Divine Sorrows, would ye look at her at her age, and the young fella she's goin' out with now.
Oh, that's her new toy friend, luv.

Would ye look at the two of them. That wan is worse than a hoover, she'd pick up anything.

... and she says he told her that he thinks she's a great girl.
Jaysus, if he's of an age to think of her as a girl, the poor lad must be a bit feeble.

I hear young Jimmy has lost the girl friend.
Oh, he must have forgotten where he laid her.

Well, he was going out with one of the Royalettes, but I heard that the show only ran for five nights.

I'm fed up of them. I'm forgettin' all men, Mary.
So am I, luv, so am I. I'm for gettin' them as soon as I can.

Mary, luv, I'd say you were up all night, your eyes are like two burnt holes in a blanket. Those aren't bags under your eyes, it's a whole set of luggage.

... and now me nose is bleedin' too this month, Bridie.
Jaysus, if it isn't one part of ye, it's another.

Well, I'll tell ye, Maisie, that crowd livin' over me must be goin' around the place on roller skates. It's like livin' under a bowlin' alley. Not a wink of sleep did I get last night. Jaysus, I tell ye, it's a bleedin' weekend all the week with them.

Well, I got such a shock. It put the wind up me so far that I'm not sure if it still hasn't come down.
Oh, I know the feeling, luv. Isn't it like the ESB running thru ye?

Mary, that cuppa tea is terrible, it's worse than drinking cold Jeyes Fluid.

I'm fed up of this stall, I don't know why I bother working for ye.
Listen, luv, it's not why ye work for me, but when.

Jaysus, Bridie, there's no one comin' near me today at all. I've been standin' still for so long that ye could strike a match on me.

Oh sorry, luv, what was that ye said? For a minute there I was away in the arms of the Murphys. I was havin' a doze here to pass away the time while I was awake.

I'm addin' up wrong all day. I must get the lead in me pencil sharpened.

Well, them bleedin' flies — Christ, wouldn't they buzz off and find themselves a nice dog shite and leave me misfortunate produce alone.

Jaysus, them flies, I could do with a collander over me head, Maisie. It'd keep off the flies, shade me eyes from the sun and let in the air at the same time.

Them bleedin' mice at home, I think I'll have to have the Corpo in to them.
Why, luv, are you thinking of havin' them trained or wha'?

Me horse, it was a dead cert, but when I backed it, it turned out more dead than a cert.

... and are ye worried about yer grocery bill at all, missus, says oul' Flanagan to me?
Well, Mr Flanagan, there's no use in the two of us worrying, says I.

Oul' Flanagan says that business is so bad this year, that even the people who never pay him don't buy anything.

Bridie, can ye give us the lend of a quid?
For what?
Jaysus, I want to open up a supermarket, don't I?

I caught that young fella tryin' to feck an orange off the stall. I'm tellin' ye that fella is livin' off his wits.
All I can say is the poor lad must be half starved.

God, you're in great humour today, Sally. You've been a walkin' joke there all morning.
Oh indeed, luv, but I'll tell ye something for nothing — with the state of mind I'm in I'm laughin' to stop meself from cryin'.

Hey, yer man must think I'm a teddy bear — he just asked me if I've got cotton wool balls.

Jaysus, that fella keeps asking me the time — he must think I'm bleedin' Big Ben.
Maybe, Bridie, it's the movement of your hands.

Jaysus, if yer man doesn't stop smilin' at me, me apron will start to fade.

Jaysus, Mary, I'm wall-fallin'. It's so long since I've eaten, me stomach thinks me throat is cut.

Maisie, if you can't give me your word of honour will ye at least give me your promise?

Oh, I wish I was outa' here for good. I'd love to go to Hollywood where you could live happily and get married ever after.

● WEATHER ●

Such a dreadful mornin', luv, it looks as if it's been up all night. And that bleedin' sun, all shine and no heat.

Mary, wasn't it very cold last night? Me teeth were chattering for an hour.
So were mine, luv, even though they were on the table at the time.

It's as cold and stiff as a frozen snot, I'd love to get something nice and hot inside me. What would ye suggest?
Well, luv, I don't think I could say it out loud with all these people around.

Jaysus, luv, it's so cold today ye'd need yer terminal underwear on.

Some Dublin Slang

• SLANG PHRASES •

You big long drink of water. *Insult, particularly to a tall thin person.*

She is very old, but she has all her facilities. *Faculties.*

She's like a bag of cats. *In very bad humour.*

Go home and tell your mother to get married. *Common put down.*

He'd shit in your parlour and charge you for it. *A mean person.*

He's a bit of a molly. *Effeminate.*

That fella is as wide as a gate. *Sharp mind, cute.*

May you die roarin' like Doran's ass! *A curse.*

I wanna do me number two. *A child who wants to go to the toilet.*

He'd talk the teeth off a saw. *A person who talks non-stop.*

That fella's a right cur. *An insult.*

He's gone for his tea. *A person who has died.*

Your eyes are bigger nor your belly. *A greedy person.*

He bet him as black as a mourning coach. *Description of a beating.*

There was laughin' and curran'y cake and talkin' to girls. *A good party.*

Don't be actin' the maggot. *Messing.*

They're like arse-holes, sure everybody has them. *When there is a plentiful supply.*

He hadn't a flitter on him. *No clothes.*

You have no call to that. *No claim or right.*

I wouldn't bother me arse about that. *Something not worth considering.*

Goin' around like a constipated greyhound. *Down in the dumps, glum.*

As fit as a cello. *Even fitter than a fiddle.*

As scarce as hobby-horse manure. *Does not exist.*

I will in me hat. *I won't do it.*

It was the rale Ally Dally. *The genuine article.*

He'd live in your ear and sublet your ear-drum. *A mean fellow.*

If bull-shit was music, that fellow'd be a brass band. *Talks a load of rubbish.*

He's like the barber's cat, full of wind and piss. *All talk and no action.*

She's as white as a maggot. *Dead.*

As fat as a bishop.

There's no use in bein' iggerant unless you can show it. *A retort.*

One wit more and he'd be a half-wit. *Being too funny by half.*

He wouldn't give you the steam off his piss. *A mean fellow.*

He has an eye like a stinkin' eel. *He watches everything.*

Do you want your snot broke? *Are you looking for a fight?*

Do you want your eye dyed? *Are you looking for a fight? (a black eye)*

She has a face like the back of a cab. *Ugly.*

That fellow'll be late for his own funeral. *Slow.*

That one is so mean she puts the butter on the bread with a feather and takes it off again with a razor. *Exceptionally mean.*

He thinks he's the cat's pyjamas. *He thinks he's perfect.*

Sure it was like throwin' apples into an orchard. *Doing something stupid.*

I nearly had a canary. *I was angry, and nearly exploded.*

A little fart of a fella. *Small.*

I knew him when he hadn't an arse to his trousers. *Well off now but comes from a poor background like myself.*

She's no oil-painting. *Not very pretty.*

He was fit to be tied. *Mad, angry.*

He'd lick it off a sore leg. *Fond of drink.*

She'd eat you out of house and home. *Big appetite.*

It gave me the hump. *Bored me.*

Cold and stiff, like a frozen snot. *A person who is cold.*

There's only one head bigger than Joe's and that's Bray Head. *Self opinionated.*

He ran like a hairyman. *Very fast.*

As small as a mouse's diddy. *Tiny.*

He's half a cocker and half a conger eel. *A mongrel dog.*

That fella'd skin a fart. *Do anything for money.*

Where would ye be goin' an' no bell on your bike. *A sly but jovial way of asking for information.*

As pretty as Pamela. *Lord Edward Fizgerald's wife, maybe!*

• SLANG TERMS •

aytin' house *restaurant*
babby *a baby*
banjaxed *so drunk – unable to walk*
beaver *a beard*
bellier *a flat dive*
biff *a slap (in school)*
bobby *policeman*
bowsy *scoundrel*
bowler *a dog*
boxing the fox *robbing an orchard*
bronical *bronchial*
bum freezer *a short coat*
bummer *a borrower*
burgoo *porridge*
Caddy *Catechism*
chaney *broken bit of delf*

chiseler *child (affectionate term)*
clickin' mots *chasing girls*
clod *a penny*
cog *to copy*
combo *football practice*
crock *an old bicycle or car*
crulety *cruelty*
cut *appearance*
dawny *sick-looking*
decko *a look*
deuce *twopence*
dickied out *dressed up*
diddy *breast*
doorsteps *thick slices of bread*
earwigger *eavesdropper*
ecker *home exercise*
fanner *a fellow who won't work*
feck *to steal*
fluthered *happily drunk*
folleyed *followed*
fudge *a farthing*
gardener *Park Ranger*
gargle *drink*
geyser *a cat*
gollier *a spittle*
gouger *a low ignorant lout*
goyno *money*
great gas *good fun*
greg *to tantalise*
grush *money thrown*
hardchaw *tough guy*
hardroot *a devil-may-care*
haut *hit (past tense)*
hop *a dance*
jow off *buzz off*
ler on *to pretend*
longers *long trousers*
Lord Muck *someone living above his station*
lugged *dragged by the ear*
make *a ha'penny*
Mary Hick *overdressed in very poor taste*
me oul' fella *my father*
me oul' wan *my mother*
mebs *marbles*
mickey dazzler *a natty dresser*

mongler *mongrel*
mosey *a stroll*
mot *woman or girlfriend*
musicianer *musician*
nark *to complain*
not the full shilling *mad*
on the jare *mitching*
ould bar *a song*
oul' rip *a spiteful person*
oul' wan *a woman*
out on gur *staying away from home*
pie-eyed *so drunk – unable to see*
rozzer *a policeman*
rucky up *a row*
ruggy *a row*
scut *a small fellow*

slug *a mouthful*
spar *boxing stance*
spifflicated *hopelessly drunk*
stabber *cigarette butt*
stag *to betray*
stand out *to fight*
stookawn *a fool*
swalleyed *swallowed*
toucher *a borrower*
whitenin' *whiting*
wing *a penny*
would a duck swim? *a reply when the answer to a question is obvious (also:* is the Pope a Catholic?*)*
young wan *a girl*

Other books from The O'Brien Press

ARCHAEOLOGY

Viking Dublin Exposed - The Wood Quay Saga, *Ed. John Bradley*. The importance of Viking Dublin and the contemporary controversy about Wood Quay.

ARCHITECTURE AND ENVIRONMENT

Buildings of Irish Towns - Treasures of Everyday Architecture, *Patrick and Maura Shaffrey*. A study and celebration of local architecture, with full-colour, award-winning illustrations and b/w photos.

Irish Countryside Buildings - Everyday Architecture in the Rural Landscape, *Patrick and Maura Shaffrey*. A companion volume to *Towns*. Together they form the first countrywide survey of Ireland's local architecture.

Steps and Steeples - Cork at the Turn of the Century, *Colm Lincoln*. Victorian Cork and environs. Lavishly illustrated with period photos.

ART

Irish Art Heritage - from 2000 B.C., *Hilary Gilmore*. Beautifully illustrated book on design in Irish art through the centuries.

BIOGRAPHY AND MEMOIRS

Voices of Ireland *Donncha Ó Dúlaing*. Interviews with people some of whom are already part of Irish history, some from the art world - and a few surprises.

Me Jewel and Darlin' Dublin *Éamonn MacThomáis*. The history and way of life of old Dublin - Dubliners' favourite book about Dublin.

The Labour and the Royal *Éamonn MacThomáis*. The wartime years and after (1942-52) in Dublin.

Gur Cake and Coal Blocks *Éamonn MacThomáis*. The fantastic, forgotten lore of MacThomáis's youth.

Janey Mack Me Shirt is Black *Éamonn MacThomáis*. Street rhymes, stories and incidents from Dublin's past.

Your Dinner's Poured Out *Paddy Crosbie*. Dublin 1913-1930, a personal account by a superb storyteller.

CHILDREN

Faery Nights/Oícheanta Sí - Stories on Ancient Irish Festivals, *Micheál macLiammóir*. Stories of magic and mystery, with illustrations by the author.

Jimeen - An Irish Comic Classic, *Pádraig Ó Siochfhradha*. A favourite character of Irish children since the 1920s - for the first time in English.

The Lucky Bag - Classic Irish Children's Stories, *Ed. Dillon, Donlon, Egan, Fallon*.